Venus

by
Melanie Chrismer

Children's Press
An Imprint of Scholastic Inc.
New York Toronto London Auckland Sydney
Mexico City New Delhi Hong Kong
Danbury, Connecticut

These content vocabulary word builders
are for grades 1–2.

Consultant: Michelle Yehling, Astronomy Education Consultant

Photo Credits:

Photographs © 2008: Corbis Images: 19 (Wolfgang Kaehler), 7 (Roy Morsch), 4 bottom left, 15 top (Galen Rowell); NASA: 5 top left, 5 top right, 15 bottom; Peter Arnold Inc./Astrofoto: back cover, 5 bottom left, 9; Photo Researchers, NY: 4 top, 11 top (European Space Agency/SPL), 13 (Mark Marten/NASA), 1, 2, 5 bottom right, 11 bottom, 23 right (NASA/Science Source); PhotoDisc/Getty Images via SODA: cover, 17, 23 left.

Illustration Credits:

Illustration page 4 bottom right by Pat Rasch   Illustration pages 20–21 by Greg Harris

Book Design: Simonsays Design!
Book Production: The Design Lab

Library of Congress Cataloging-in-Publication Data
Chrismer, Melanie.
Venus / by Melanie Chrismer.—Updated ed.
    p. cm.—(Scholastic news nonfiction readers)
Includes bibliographical references and index.
ISBN-13: 978-0-531-14755-9 (lib. bdg.)   978-0-531-14770-2 (pbk.)
ISBN-10: 0-531-14755-X (lib. bdg.)   0-531-14770-3 (pbk.)
1. Venus (Planet)—Juvenile literature. I. Title.
QB621.C57 2007
523.42—dc22   2006102780

All rights reserved. Published by Children's Press, an imprint of Scholastic Inc.
Published simultaneously in Canada. Printed in the United States of America. 44

SCHOLASTIC, CHILDREN'S PRESS, and associated logos are trademarks
and/or registered trademarks of Scholastic Inc.

1 2 3 4 5 6 7 8 9 10 R 17 16 15 14 13 12 11 10 09 08

3 1984 00292 5921

CONTENTS

WORD HUNT

Look for these words as you read. They will be in **bold**.

clouds
(kloudz)

mountains
(**moun**-tuhnz)

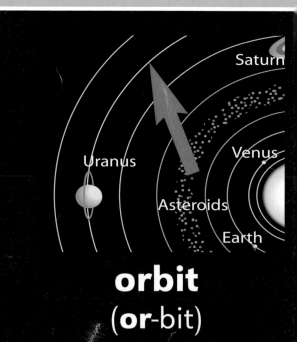

orbit
(**or**-bit)

4

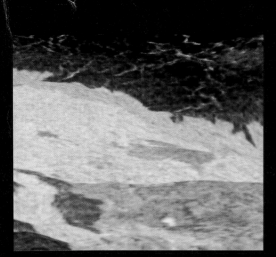

lava
(**lah**-vuh)

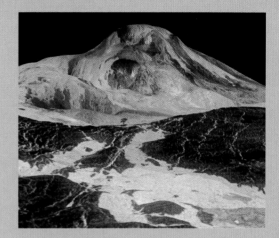

Maat Mons
(maht monz)

solar system
(**soh**-lur **siss**-tuhm)

Venus
(**vee**-nuhs)

Venus!

It is fun to fly a kite on Earth.

But can you go fly a kite on **Venus**?

No. You cannot go to Venus at all.

Flying kites on Earth is fun.

Venus is the second planet in our **solar system**.

All of the planets in the solar system travel around the Sun on a path called an **orbit**.

Venus is closer to the Sun than Earth is. It is hotter on Venus than on Earth.

Venus

Earth

Venus is called Earth's sister. They are the same in many ways.

They are almost the same size.

They are both made out of rock and metal.

They both have **clouds**.

Earth

Venus

11

Venus and Earth are different, too.

The clouds on Earth are made of water.

The clouds on Venus are made of acid.

The acid in the clouds on
Venus would burn your skin.

Venus and Earth have **mountains** and volcanoes.

The highest mountain on Earth is Mount Everest.

The highest mountain on Venus is Maxwell Montes. It is almost 7 miles (11.5 kilometers) high.

One of the highest volcanoes on Venus is **Maat Mons**.

The highest volcano on Earth is Ojos del Salado. It is more than 4 miles (6.5 km) high.

**Mount Everest is 5 ¹/₂ miles
(9 km) high.**

**Maat Mons is 5 ¹/₂ miles
(9 km) high.**

Almost all of Venus is covered with **lava**. Lava is hot melted rock or melted rock that has cooled and hardened.

Almost all of Earth is covered with water.

oceans

No, you cannot fly a kite on Venus.

But on Earth you can do many things.

You can fly a kite. You can swim in the ocean, and you can be happy you do not live on Venus!

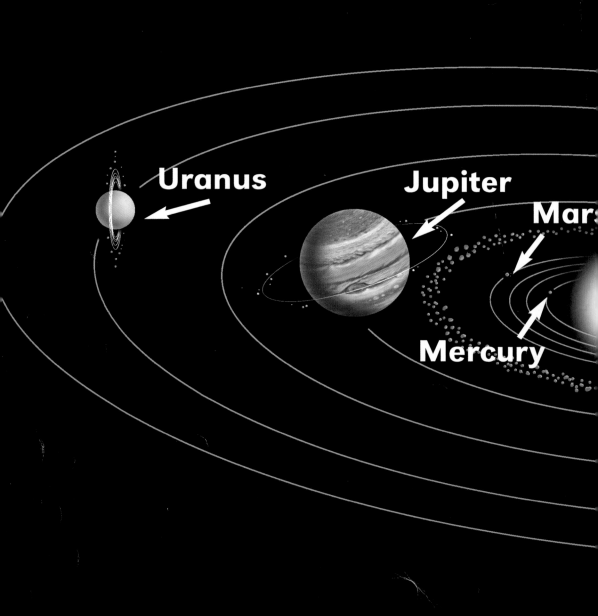

Uranus

Jupiter

Mars

Mercury

VENUS
IN OUR SOLAR SYSTEM

Sun

Venus

Saturn

Earth

Neptune

YOUR NEW WORDS

clouds (kloudz) groups of liquid droplets that can be seen above the surface of a planet

lava (**lah**-vuh) hot melted rock or melted rock that has cooled and hardened

Maat Mons (maht monz) one of the highest volcanoes on Venus

mountains (**moun**-tuhnz) high pieces of land

orbit (**or**-bit) the path an object takes around another object

solar system (**soh**-lur **siss**-tuhm) the group of planets, moons, and other things that travel around the Sun

Venus (**vee**-nuhs) a planet named after the Roman goddess of beauty and love

Earth and Venus

A year is how long it takes a planet to go around the Sun.

 1 Earth year =365 days

 1 Venus year =225 Earth days

A day is how long it takes a planet to turn one time.

 1 Earth day = 24 hours

 1 Venus day = 5,834 Earth hours or 243 Earth days

A moon is an object that circles a planet.

 Earth has 1 moon.

 Venus has no moons.

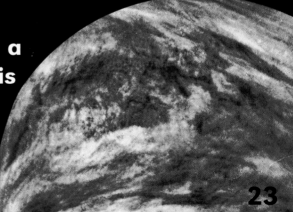

Astronomers have found a lava river on Venus that is more than 4,000 miles (6,437 km) long.

INDEX

FIND OUT MORE
Book:
Cole, Michael D. *Venus: The Second Planet*. Berkeley Heights,
NJ: Enslow Publishers, Inc., 2001.

Web site:
Solar System Exploration
http://sse.jpl.nasa.gov/planets/

MEET THE AUTHOR

Melanie Chrismer grew up near NASA in Houston, Texas.
She loves math and science and has written thirteen books
for children. To write her books, she visited NASA where she
floated in the zero-gravity trainer called the Vomit Comet.
She says, "it is the best roller coaster ever!"